W9-ADW-396

Sheep of Fools

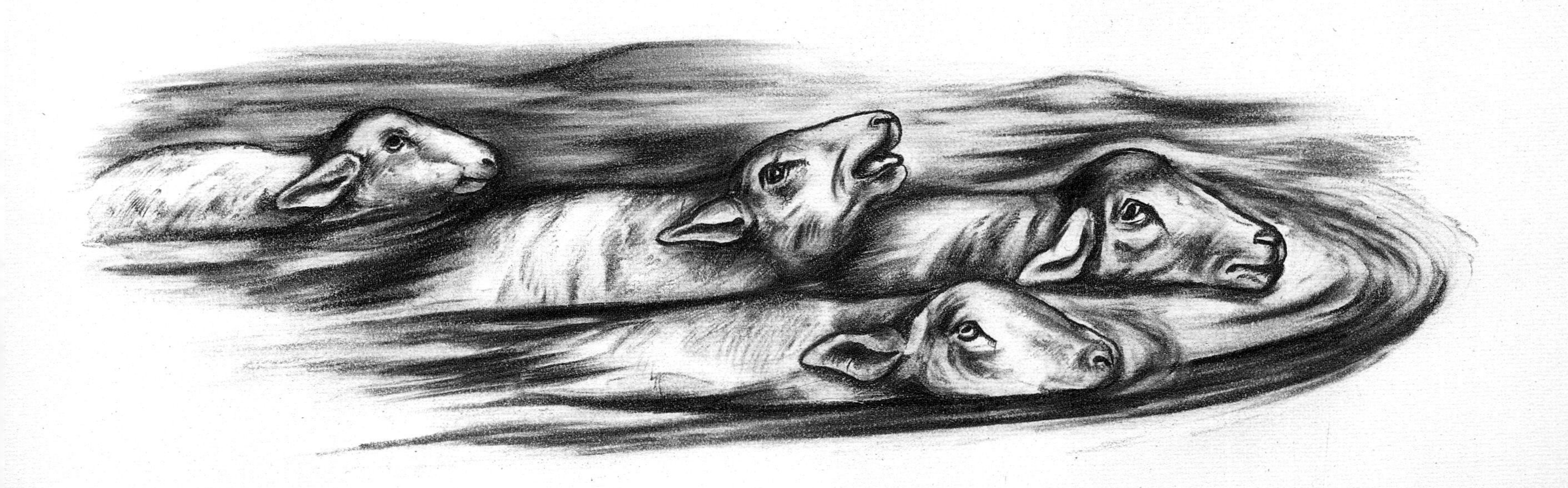

THIS BOOK IS DEDICATED TO PATTY MARK AND ALL ANIMAL LIBERATION ACTIVISTS

STORY: Sue Coe and Judith Brody
ARTWORK: Sue Coe
EDITOR: Monte Beauchamp
DESIGN/ART DIRECTION/PRODUCTION: Monte Beauchamp
PUBLISHER: Fantagraphics Books

Fantagraphics Books, 7563 Lake City Way NE, Seattle, WA 98115
Printed in China

WWW.FANTAGRAPHICS.COM

ISBN 1-56097-6608
First Fantagraphics Books Edition: August 2005

Sheep of Fools

... A Song Cycle For Five Voices

Sue Coe & Judith Brody

A BLAB! PICTO-NOVELETTE • PUBLISHED BY FANTAGRAPHICS • SEATTLE WASHINGTON

SONG OF THE MEDIEVAL SHEPHERD*

(who soon meets the Middle Man and the Venture Capitalist and learns
a lesson in interest rates and the profit motive)

Of sheep we'd sing and clover's rings in pastures green and gold;
of days gone by, where shepherds lie and picnic with the fold.
Before the farm turned factory, the shepherd turned to cog,
he worked alone, long years ago, that sheepman and his dog.

So peaceful there, without a care — the change has been immense.
Our fateful, once bucolic hours, exchanged that sense for cents.

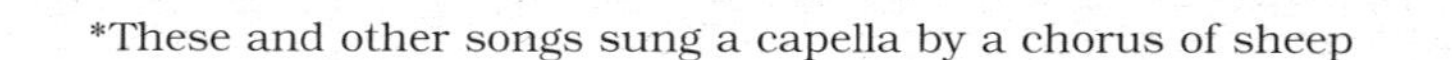

*These and other songs sung a capella by a chorus of sheep

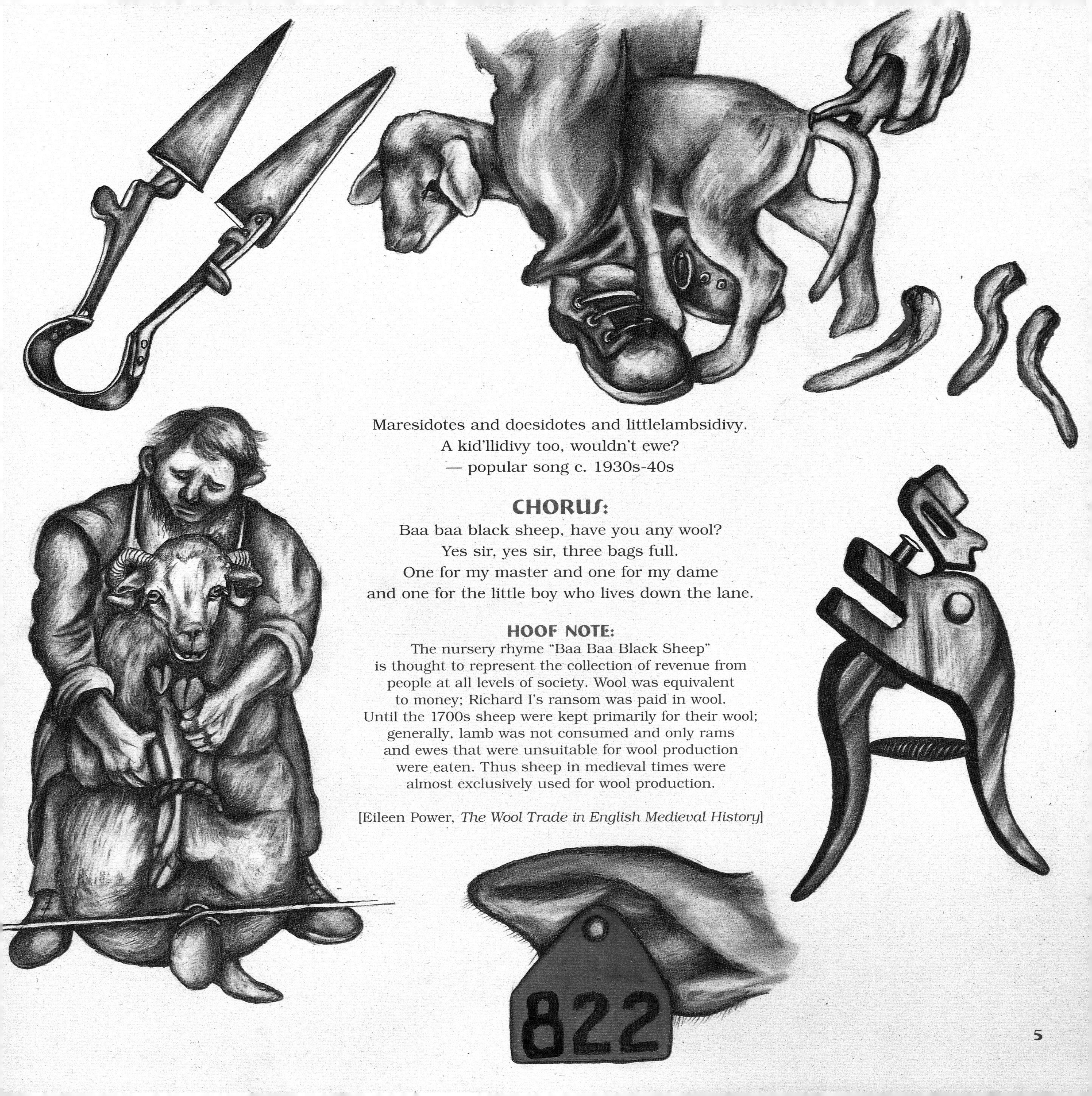

Maresidotes and doesidotes and littlelambsidivy.
A kid'llidivy too, wouldn't ewe?
— popular song c. 1930s-40s

CHORUS:

Baa baa black sheep, have you any wool?
Yes sir, yes sir, three bags full.
One for my master and one for my dame
and one for the little boy who lives down the lane.

HOOF NOTE:

The nursery rhyme "Baa Baa Black Sheep" is thought to represent the collection of revenue from people at all levels of society. Wool was equivalent to money; Richard I's ransom was paid in wool. Until the 1700s sheep were kept primarily for their wool; generally, lamb was not consumed and only rams and ewes that were unsuitable for wool production were eaten. Thus sheep in medieval times were almost exclusively used for wool production.

[Eileen Power, *The Wool Trade in English Medieval History*]

SONG OF THE VENTURE CAPITALIST

(who figures out how to take on a little risk for a large gain, and who owes a debt of gratitude to the Knights Templar for passing on what they learned about banking at the Crusades)

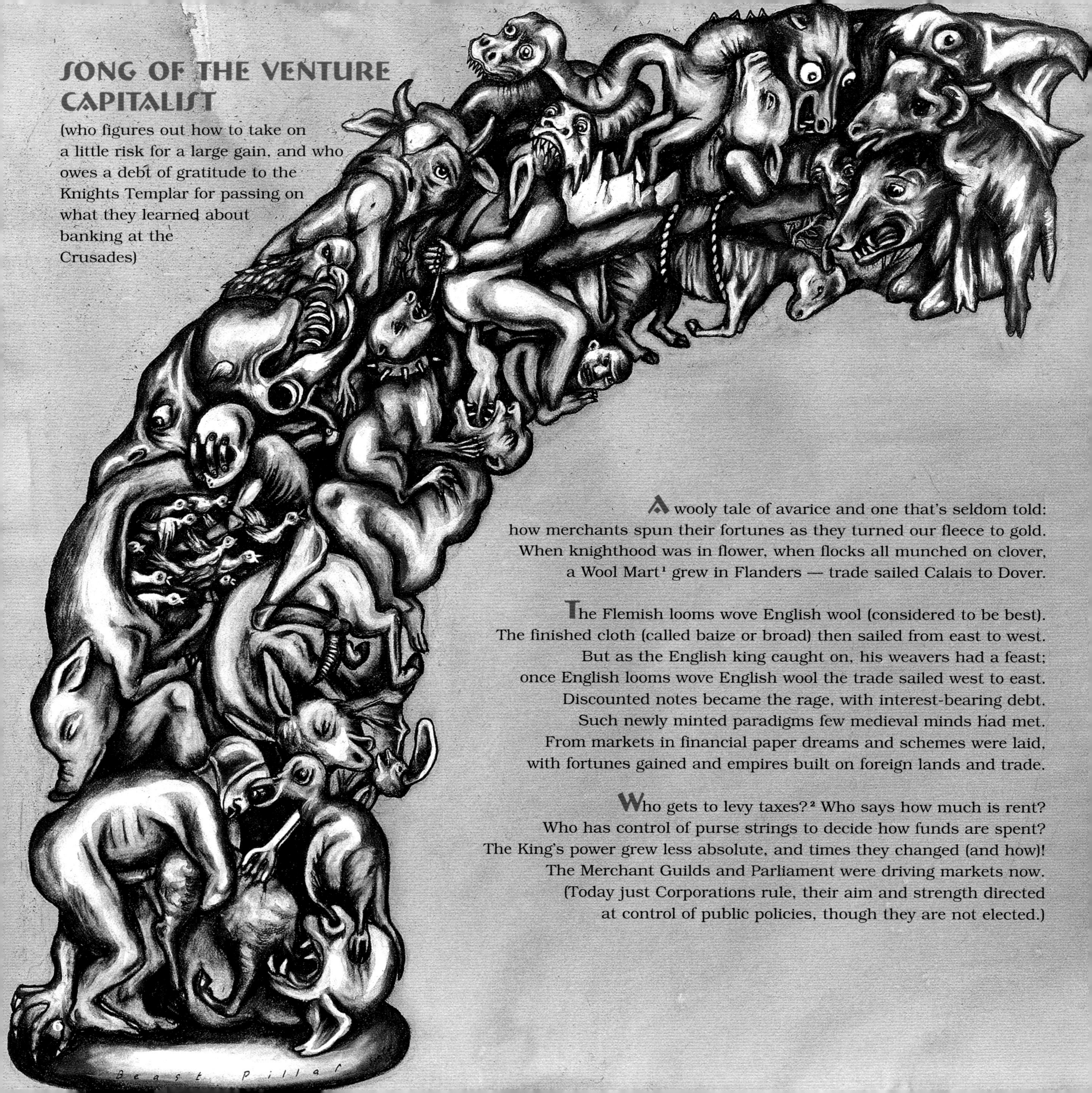

A wooly tale of avarice and one that's seldom told:
how merchants spun their fortunes as they turned our fleece to gold.
When knighthood was in flower, when flocks all munched on clover,
a Wool Mart[1] grew in Flanders — trade sailed Calais to Dover.

The Flemish looms wove English wool (considered to be best).
The finished cloth (called baize or broad) then sailed from east to west.
But as the English king caught on, his weavers had a feast;
once English looms wove English wool the trade sailed west to east.
Discounted notes became the rage, with interest-bearing debt.
Such newly minted paradigms few medieval minds had met.
From markets in financial paper dreams and schemes were laid,
with fortunes gained and empires built on foreign lands and trade.

Who gets to levy taxes?[2] Who says how much is rent?
Who has control of purse strings to decide how funds are spent?
The King's power grew less absolute, and times they changed (and how)!
The Merchant Guilds and Parliament were driving markets now.
(Today just Corporations rule, their aim and strength directed
at control of public policies, though they are not elected.)

HOOF NOTE:

1. Known as the ENGLISH COMPANY OF THE MERCHANTS OF THE STAPLE, by the 15th century the Wool Mart in Calais was a quasi-monopoly that set the price and determined who could buy and sell wool.

2. To raise funds for wars in the 13th and 14th centuries, taxes were levied and paid in sacks of wool. The balance of power and working relationships among the Parliament, merchants and King evolved in relation to wool. To this day, the British Lord Chancellor, who presides in the House of Lords, is said to "sit on the woolsack," or to be "appointed to the woolsack." The sack is a large square bag of wool, without back or arms, and covered with red cloth. It serves as a reminder of the source of Britain's wealth and power.

Fast forward past the Renaissance; the British Empire branching had claimed Australia's virgin soil for convicts and sheep ranching. Conditions were most fortunate, despite a dearth of rain. We sheep were fruitful, multiplied, then shipped off to Bahrain (and other Mideast ports of call that wouldn't take sheep frozen but must import their sheep alive, across the vast, deep ocean).

HOOF NOTE:

TRANSPORTATION: punishment in the form of banishment to a term of slave labor in a British colony from 7 years to life for offenses that were most frequently the result of petty crimes and poverty. Established in 1717 and continued as a practice until 1868. In 1783, with the loss of England's American colonies as a convict dumping ground, prisons in England rapidly filled; old ships at anchor termed 'hulks' were used as floating prisons but these too were soon overcrowded. By 1786, it was decided to colonize Australia with convicts.

FIRST FLEET: historic reference to the 11 ships (8 for prisoners, 3 for stores) that brought the first British convicts to what is now the Sydney region of Australia. The crew sailed from Portsmouth England on May 13, 1787, with 586 men and 191 women convicts, with at least 44 sheep among the livestock, and arrived in Botany Bay, on January 26, 1788.

SECOND FLEET: (also known as THE DEATH FLEET, for the high mortality rate suffered during the voyage due to disease, starvation and torture.) Unlike the First Fleet's government ships and crew, this trip returned to the practice of using private contractors with experience transporting African slaves.

Now back in Georgian England, the weavers left behind were facing new industrial norms that trashed their daily grind.

They moved to town from country; from cottage to the mill; their skills at weaving cloth by hand slid swiftly down the hill.

Too many men were jobless; the pay scale dropped as well. With General Ludd, so stories say, the weavers tried to tell their side of the calamity, in anger and in song.

Machines were damaged (and rebuilt); their protests drew a throng who watched them at their trials, who saw them hung in chains, and all they got for speaking up was transport for their pains.

All we like sheep are led astray . . .
— Handel's Messiah
It is the part of a good shepherd to shear
his flock not to skin it . . .
— Latin
Without a shepherd,
sheep are not a flock . . .
— Russian saying

SONG OF THE MODERN SHEPHERD

(who has turned in his crook for a time card and now punches a clock at the factory farm)

But let's not race the story here, our tale of traveling woe. Before we're put to sea and death, let's learn just how we grow. How do a million sheep get raised? What keeps us having babies? Who tends these flocks and shears our locks and doses us for scrapies? Unasked, we've had assistance, been well-inoculated; blue-ribboned ewes at county fairs, rudely inseminated.

With human help sheep population count has now reached to the billions. If left to roam, quite on our own, we'd probably reach zillions before a Darwin deluge, in a predatory way, could sweep us all before it, and rinse most of us away. Thanks to the inbred export trade and state of the art production, sheep now have bums (would you believe?!) in need of liposuction!

The process is termed 'MULESING', a cruel deed, not bold: from breeding us for finer wool, our rear ends tend to fold, providing homes for sheep flies to lay their eggs and nest. The picture isn't pretty, and maggots will infest unless we get some treatment to discourage insect life but rather than just dip us, they slice us with a knife! The fatty folds are cut off, no hint of anesthetic. All trussed up there, hooves in the air, we sure do look pathetic.

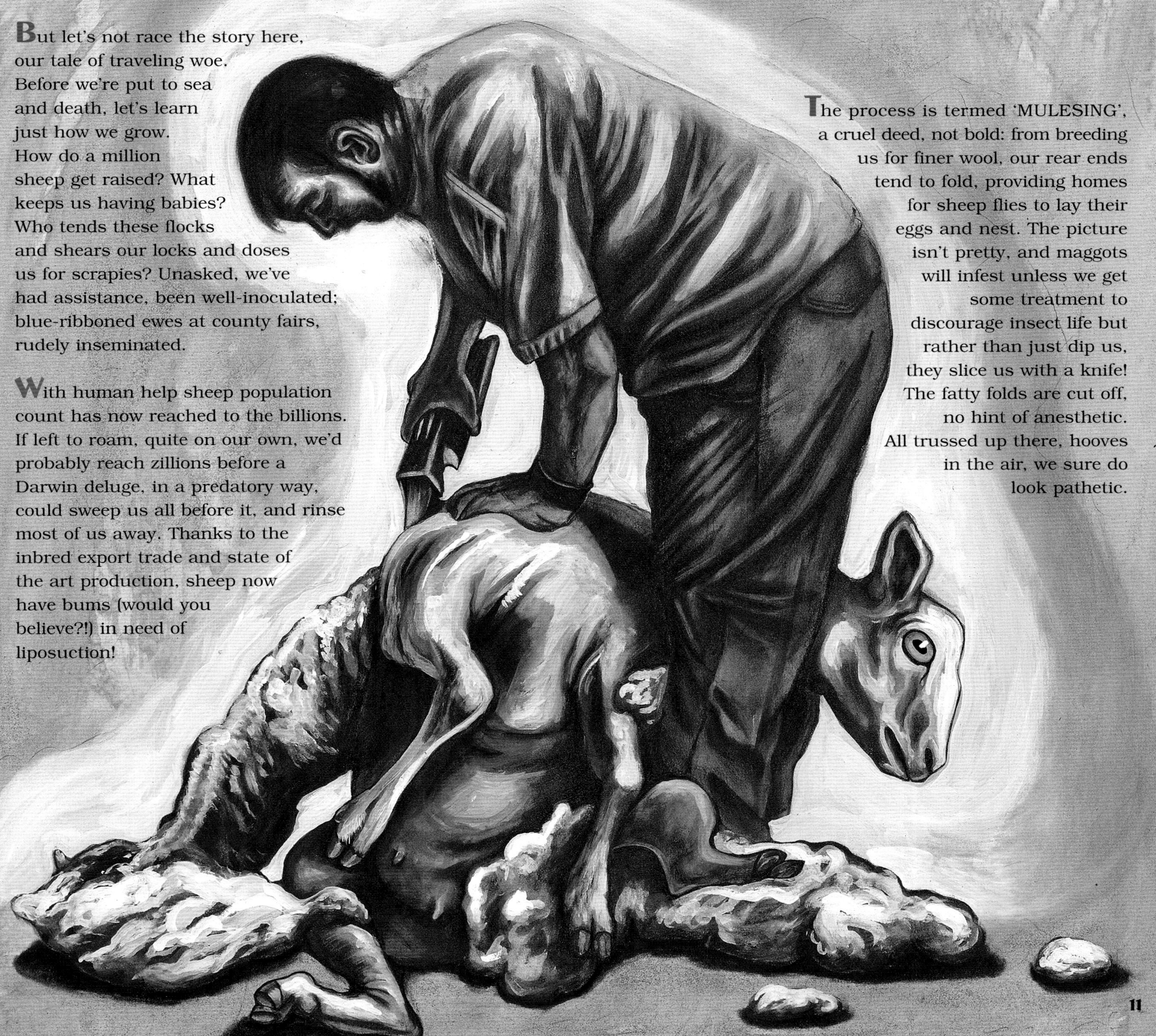

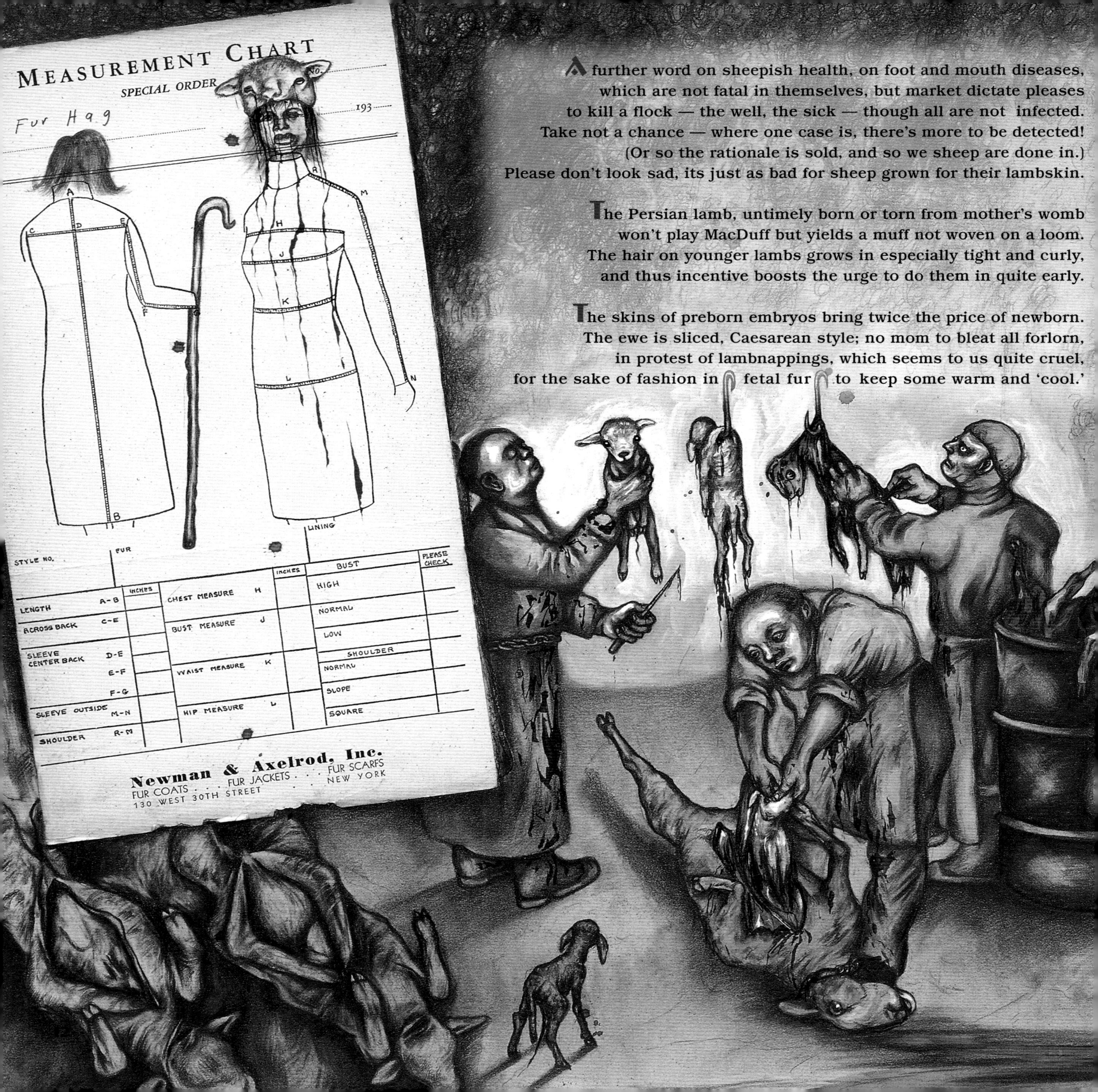

A further word on sheepish health, on foot and mouth diseases,
which are not fatal in themselves, but market dictate pleases
to kill a flock — the well, the sick — though all are not infected.
Take not a chance — where one case is, there's more to be detected!
(Or so the rationale is sold, and so we sheep are done in.)
Please don't look sad, its just as bad for sheep grown for their lambskin.

The Persian lamb, untimely born or torn from mother's womb
won't play MacDuff but yields a muff not woven on a loom.
The hair on younger lambs grows in especially tight and curly,
and thus incentive boosts the urge to do them in quite early.

The skins of preborn embryos bring twice the price of newborn.
The ewe is sliced, Caesarean style; no mom to bleat all forlorn,
in protest of lambnappings, which seems to us quite cruel,
for the sake of fashion in fetal fur to keep some warm and 'cool.'

DIOR
$25,000
$30,000
$35,000
VALENTINO
Sue Coe 07

(which don't always reach their destinations safely, much to the chagrin
not to mention the untimely demise, of their passengers and crew)

Returning to our saga of sailor sheep and men,
we now recount our journey from grass to slaughter pen.
The trip starts with a truck ride, from pastureland to port.
Long hours and dusty miles roll past; the journey's far from short.

The truck acts like an oven on sunny summer days;
heat struck we bake, no water take, without a chance to graze.
In winter cold they can't unload until we've been unstuck.
It isn't rare that by our hair we're frozen to the truck!

HOOF NOTE: By truck from their home range, sheep can travel hundreds of miles and the better part of a week without food or fresh water until they arrive at the feedlot. They are deprived of food and water prior to loading in order to reduce manure output, but the stress of travel prevents them from eating for a day or two even after they reach the feedlot. Trucks provide no shade from the sun, and no bedding. The so-called 'shy-feeders,' too stressed to eat the new diet, die of starvation. http://www.liveexportshame.com/index.htm

IMF
$
OIL
BUSH
CHENE
18

EXXON MOBILE

Days later, at the feedlot, instead of grass, a new food
to train up our digestion and get us in the right mood
for travel on the high seas, where grass is not an option.
The pellet fare is all that's there: it's starve or adaptation.
The feedlot life is stress enough, and lasts for days and days.
Far worse, the ship, a floating plot that yaws and dips and sways.

Sheep weren't made for sailors. Our skill? Grow fine wool, thick.
Put thousands on a tanker, and you know some will get sick.
'Six sea-sick sheep'? Could be a rhyme or cavalier tongue twister.
Non-fiction fact is what it is. You've grasped the gist that's put here.

A three week trip (when things went well) — 5 million a year get to go.
8% won't make it — for business costs, that's low.
It brings in $390 mil in gold Australian dollars.
No one complains, except us sheep, and no one hears our hollers.

AL-YASRAH

PRINCESS CRUISE

Four hundred thousand sheep each year
will die from stress of travel — the ships can sink
or catch on fire. No wonder sheep unravel!

In 1980 12,000 drowned — with the
Star of Shaddia sunk;
the *Farid Fares* burned 40,000,
its ancient engines junk;
the *Uniceb*, in '92, abandoned ship to fire,
and left the sheep to swim away,
and sink when they would tire.
A decade on — *Cormo Express* — they
died for lack of air.
10,000 sheep packed Auschwitz tight
all suffocated there.

But even with a voyage
where the ships don't take on water
or burn the tightly standing flocks —
it's meant to end in slaughter.

A ship, Sir, is a prison with a
chance of being drowned.
—Samuel Johnson

. . . to separate
the sheep
from the goats . . .
— Matthew 25:31-46

SONG OF THE BUTCHER

(who must accomplish the impossible: a ritual slaughter that is also compassionate)

We've travelled far across the years,
since we first grew domestic;
new hemispheres, new husbandries,
and Dolly clones genetic.
We took the place of Isaac,
for one burnt sacrifice.
Religion has its comforts,
though for us it's rarely nice.

We're still in all the holy books,
and big on holidays,
when we get killed to celebrate,
though we would rather graze.

681

Some dip a hand in fresh spilled blood and slap it on the wall to bless a newly opened shop, café or market stall. Employment counts, men earn a wage, in Middle East or West. Horrific though the process is, let's take a little test.

True-false: to kill a standing cow, it's best to blind her quick and hamstring her when she won't fall, if that will do the trick. BUZZ-ZAP! Time's up, the answer's FALSE. *Halal* this cannot be. "Not kosher" under Jewish law, *haram* to Islam, see?

Yes, ritual slaughter has its rules — supposedly it's painless, but a ritual assembly line? That's nothing short of shameless.

for slaughter

For additional information about BLAB! Picto-Novelettes,
with forthcoming titles by Camille Rose Garcia, David Sandlin, Drew Friedman, Bob Staake,
and Walter Minus, please contact: www.fantagraphics.com